I DON'T BELIEVE ONE GROWS OLDER. I THINK THAT WHAT HAPPENS EARLY ON IN LIFE IS THAT AT A CERTAIN AGE ONE STANDS STILL AND STAGNATES.

PEOPLE TO WHOM NOTHING HAS EVER HAPPENED CANNOT UNDERSTAND THE UNIMPORTANCE OF EVENTS.

WE KNOW TOO MUCH, AND ARE CONVINCED OF TOO LITTLE. OUR LITERATURE IS A SUBSTITUTE FOR RELIGION, AND SO IS OUR RELIGION.

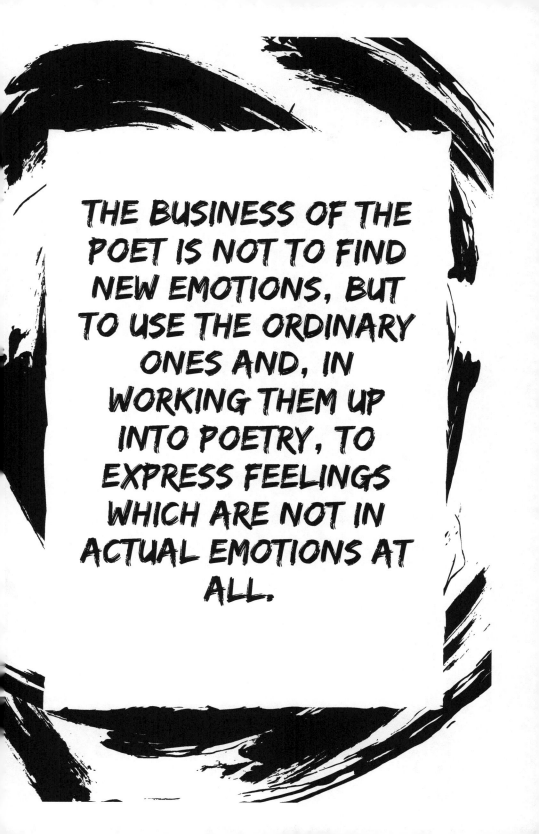

TO DO THE USEFUL THING, TO SAY THE COURAGEOUS THING, TO CONTEMPLATE THE BEAUTIFUL THING THAT IS ENOUGH FOR ONE MAN'S LIFE.

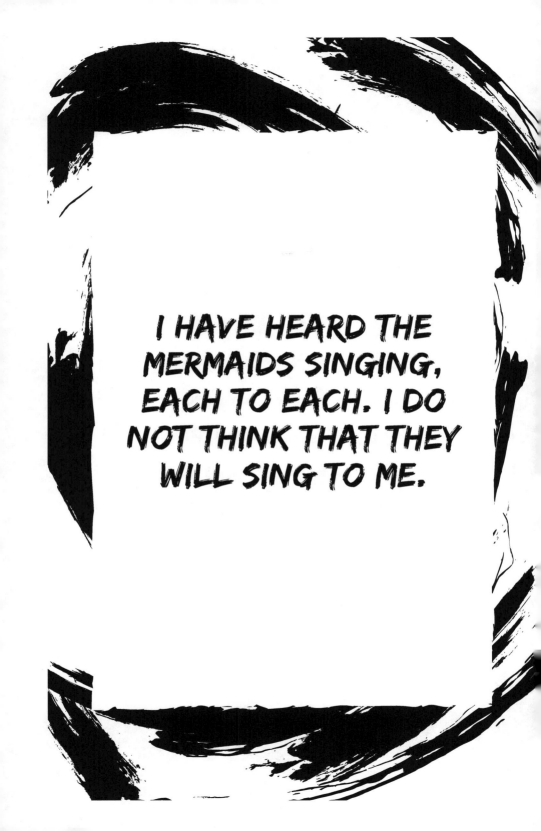

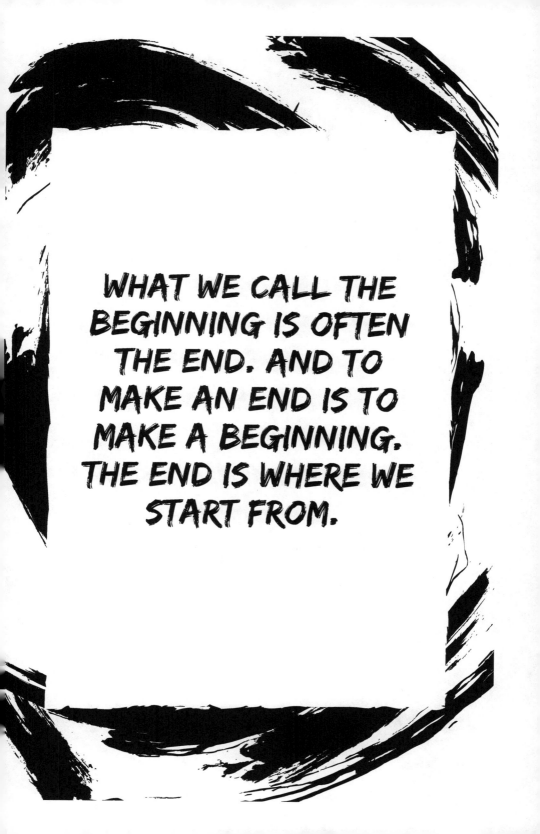

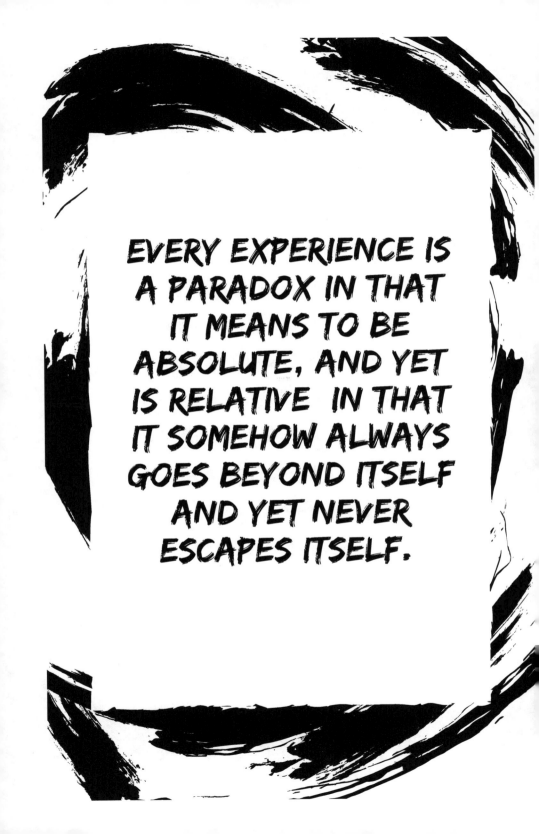

EVERY EXPERIENCE IS A PARADOX IN THAT IT MEANS TO BE ABSOLUTE, AND YET IS RELATIVE IN THAT IT SOMEHOW ALWAYS GOES BEYOND ITSELF AND YET NEVER ESCAPES ITSELF.

KNOWLEDGE IS INVARIABLY A MATTER OF DEGREE YOU CANNOT PUT YOUR FINGER UPON EVEN THE SIMPLEST DATUM AND SAY THIS WE KNOW.

ALL SIGNIFICANT TRUTHS ARE PRIVATE TRUTHS. AS THEY BECOME PUBLIC THEY CEASE TO BECOME TRUTHS THEY BECOME FACTS, OR AT BEST, PART OF THE PUBLIC CHARACTER OR AT WORST, CATCHWORDS.

OUR HIGH RESPECT FOR A WELL READ PERSON IS PRAISE ENOUGH FOR LITERATURE.

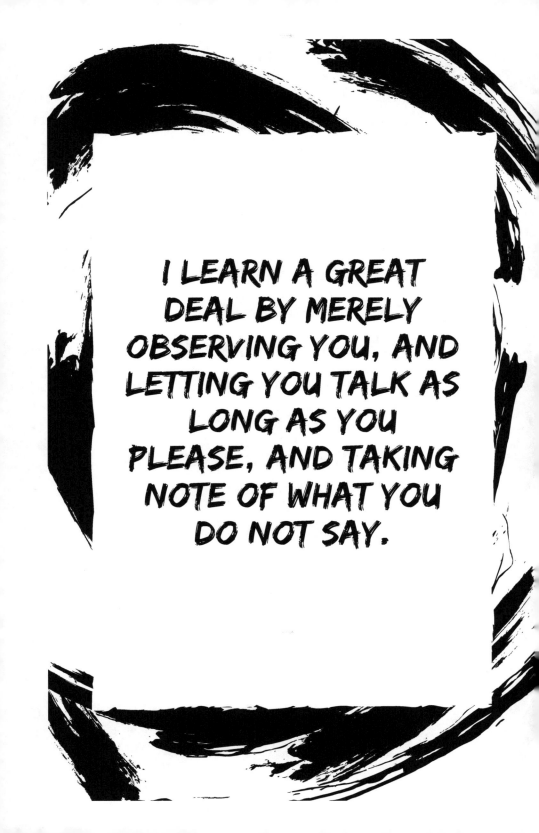

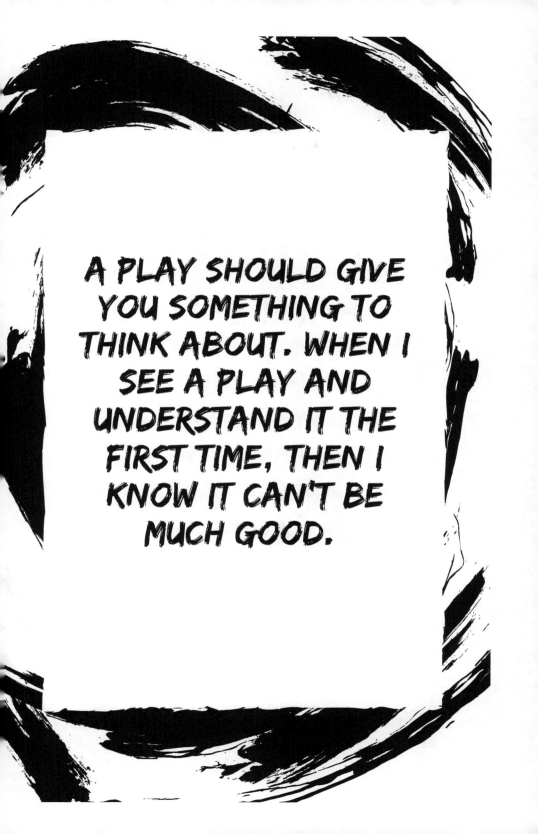

A PLAY SHOULD GIVE YOU SOMETHING TO THINK ABOUT. WHEN I SEE A PLAY AND UNDERSTAND IT THE FIRST TIME, THEN I KNOW IT CAN'T BE MUCH GOOD.

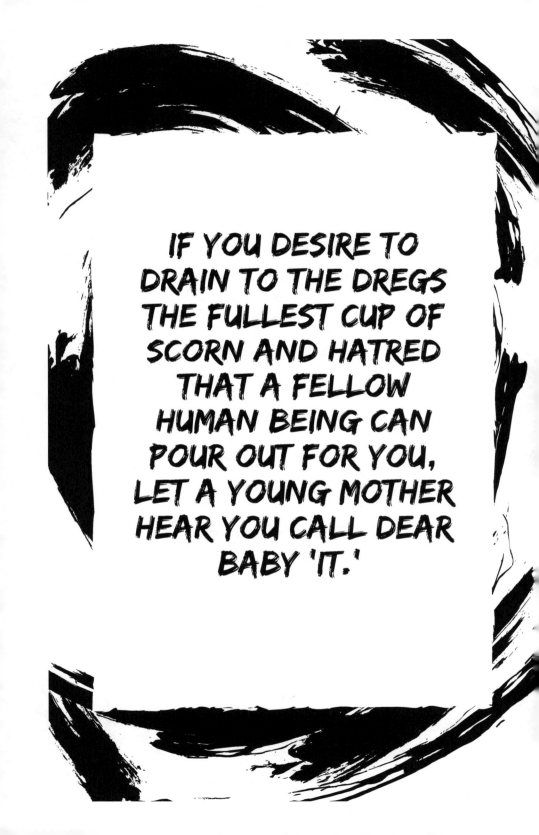

IF YOU DESIRE TO DRAIN TO THE DREGS THE FULLEST CUP OF SCORN AND HATRED THAT A FELLOW HUMAN BEING CAN POUR OUT FOR YOU, LET A YOUNG MOTHER HEAR YOU CALL DEAR BABY 'IT.'

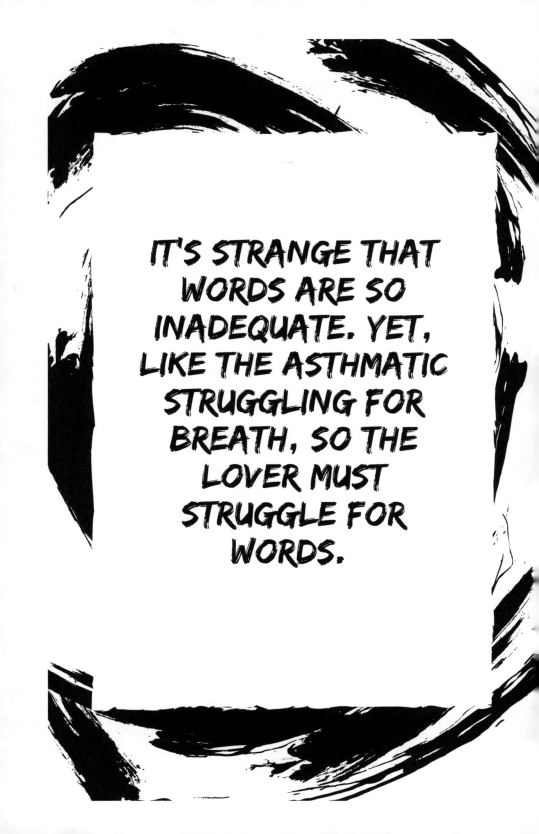

THE LAST THING ONE DISCOVERS IN COMPOSING A WORK IS WHAT TO PUT FIRST.

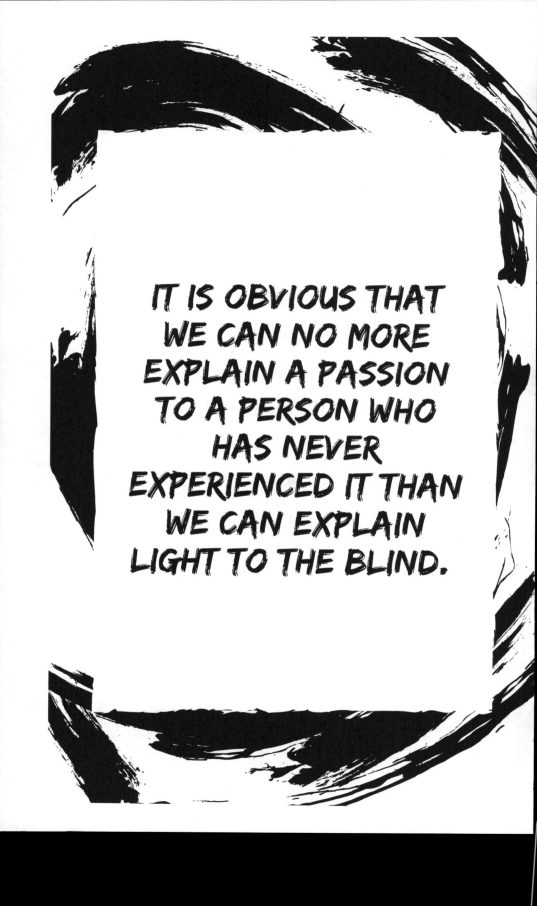

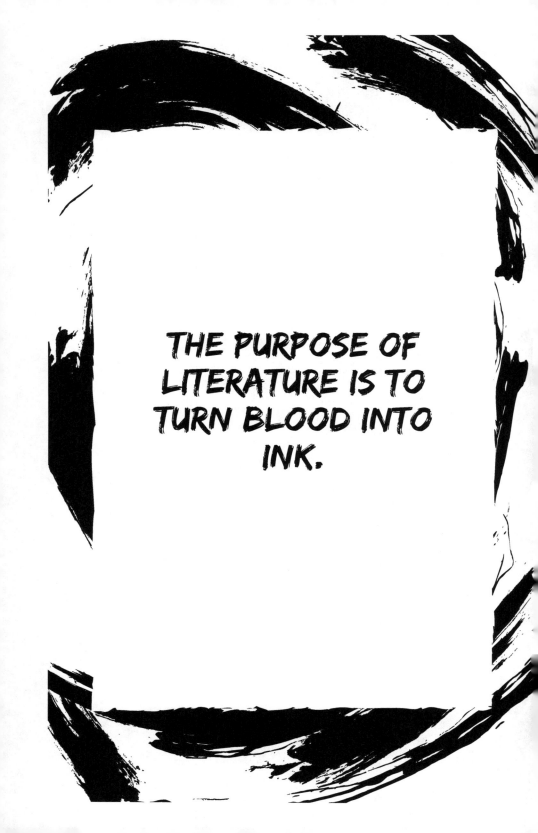

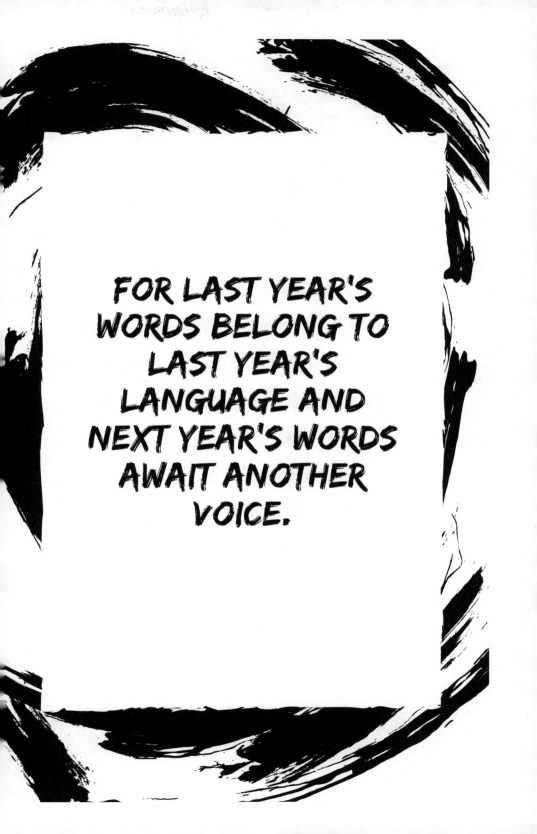

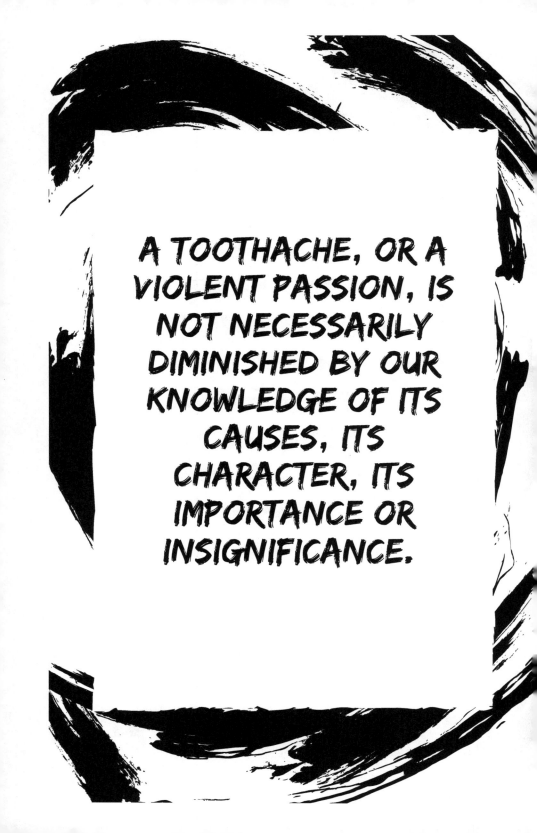

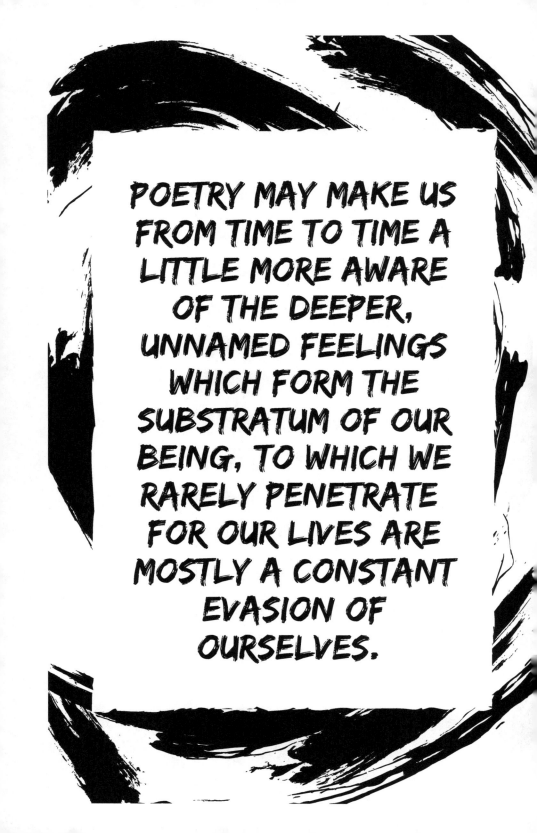

IMMATURE POETS IMITATE MATURE POETS STEAL.

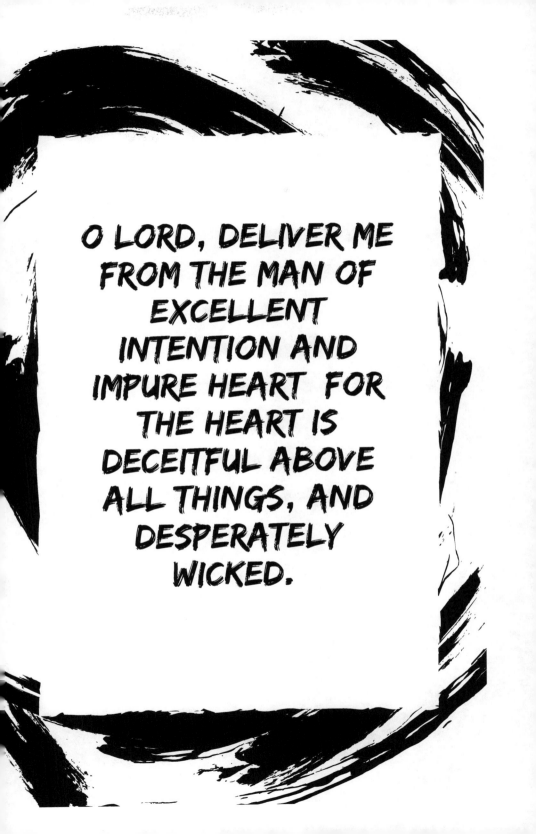

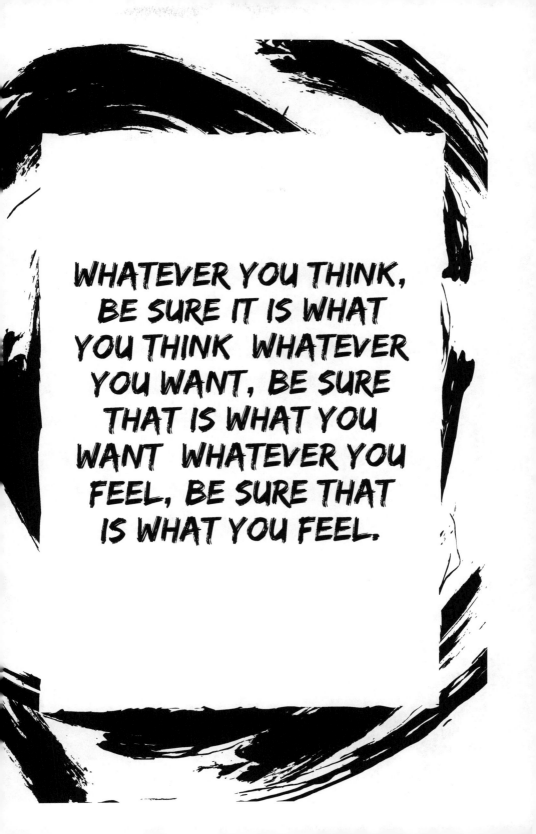

FOR LOVE WOULD BE LOVE OF THE WRONG THING THERE IS YET FAITH, BUT THE FAITH AND THE LOVE AND THE HOPE ARE ALL IN THE WAITING.

THE SOUL IS SO FAR FROM BEING A MONAD THAT WE HAVE NOT ONLY TO INTERPRET OTHER SOULS TO OURSELF BUT TO INTERPRET OURSELF TO OURSELF.

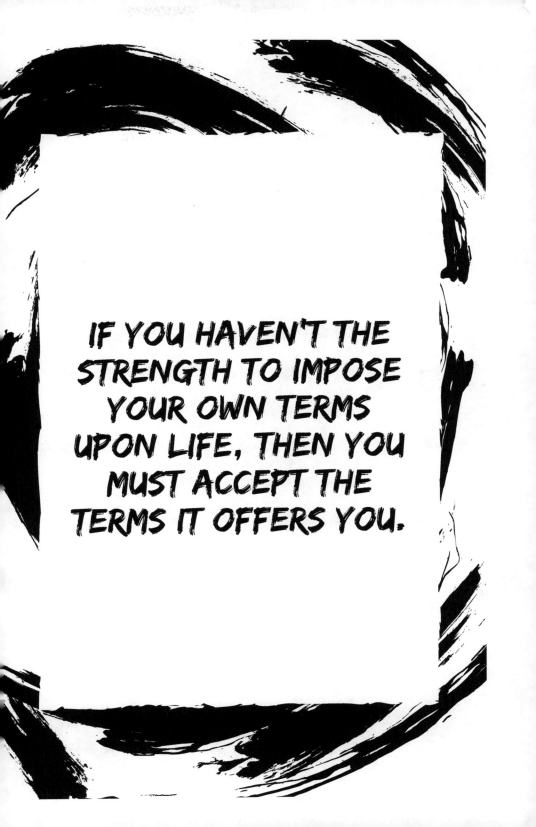

WHERE IS THE LIFE WE HAVE LOST IN LIVING? WHERE IS THE WISDOM WE HAVE LOST IN KNOWLEDGE? WHERE IS THE KNOWLEDGE WE HAVE LOST IN INFORMATION?

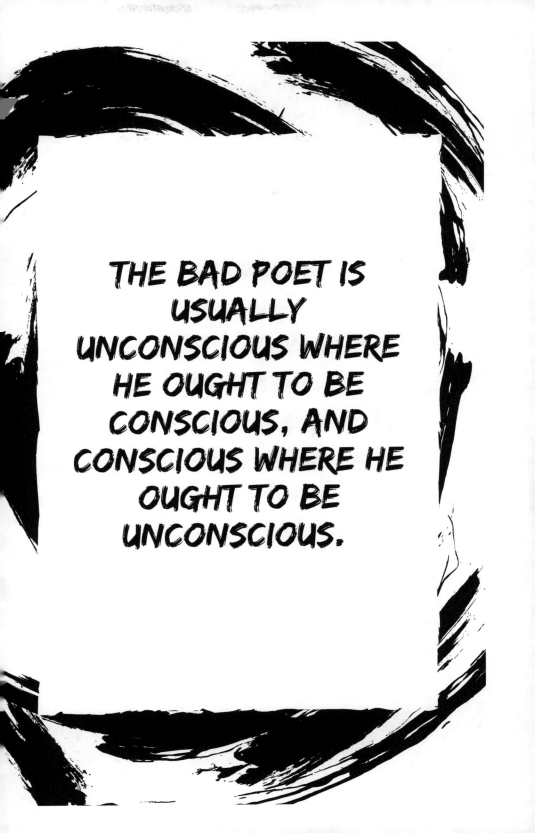

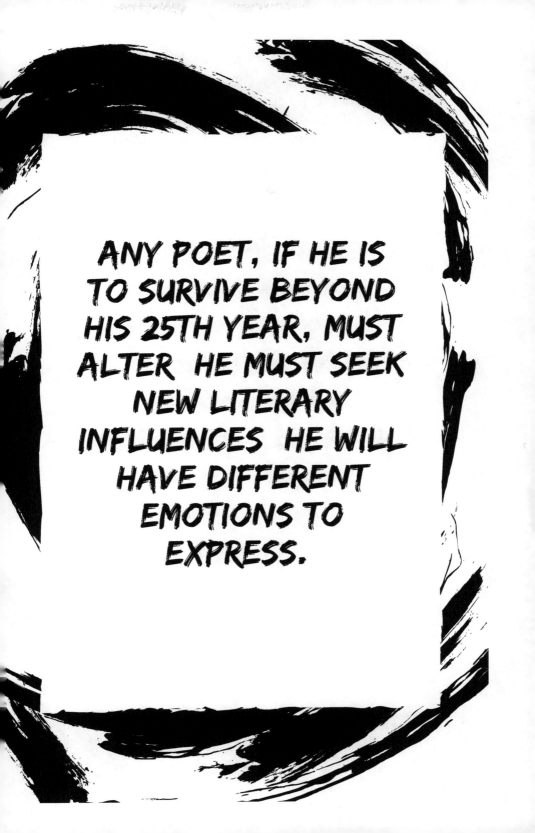

Made in the USA
Columbia, SC
09 July 2025